BEST OF FLORENCE AND TUSCANY
YOUR #1 ITINERARY PLANNER FOR WHAT TO SEE, DO, AND EAT

Wanderlust Pocket Guides

Planning a trip to Italy?

Check out our other Wanderlust Pocket Travel Guides on Amazon:

BEST OF ROME: YOUR #1 ITINERARY PLANNER FOR WHAT TO SEE, DO, AND EAT

BEST OF VENICE: YOUR #1 ITINERARY PLANNER FOR WHAT TO SEE, DO, AND EAT

BEST OF ITALY: YOUR #1 ITINERARY PLANNER FOR WHAT TO SEE, DO, AND EAT

Also available:

BEST OF JAPAN: YOUR #1 ITINERARY PLANNER FOR WHAT TO SEE, DO, AND EAT

BEST OF TOKYO: YOUR #1 ITINERARY PLANNER FOR WHAT TO SEE, DO, AND EAT

BEST OF KYOTO: YOUR #1 ITINERARY PLANNER FOR WHAT TO SEE, DO, AND EAT

Our Free Gift to You

As purchasers of this paperback copy, we are offering you an **Amazon Matchbook download** of our colored **kindle version of this book for FREE.** Go to our book's page on Amazon and select the kindle version to download.

You **do not have to own a kindle** to read the kindle version of this book. Simply download the kindle reading app on your computer, tablet, or smartphone.

"Everything about Florence seems to be colored with a mild violet, like diluted wine."

Henry James

Table of Contents

REGIONS
OF ITALY

INTRODUCTION

Established in 80 BC under the Roman Republic, Florence has practically always been an important commercial center in Italy's long history. But the beautiful city that we know today really gained its stunning landscape in the Renaissance, under the rule of the powerful Medici family, beginning in the early 1400's. Bathed under the soft Tuscan sun, the city's narrow streets, abundant world-class art, and intricate frescoed architecture, have hardly changed since then. Standing on a bridge over the Arno River, visitors often feel transported to a more romantic era, to the birth of the Renaissance era.

Known in Italian as "Firenze", the Republic of Florence was the seat of the House of Medici, a banking family and political dynasty that became enormously powerful first under its charismatic paterfamilias Cosimo de'Medici. As the family gained prominence, the family became a great patron of the artistic development of the city, most notably under the rule of Lorenzo de'Medici, also known as "Il Magnifico". In a little over 20 years (1469 to 1492), Lorenzo built Florence into the most important city-state in Italy, and the most beautiful city in all of Europe.

The Medicis' Florence − largely the Florence of today − is filled with sculptures, churches, palazzos, and art of every medium, from the most important master artists of the Renaissance. Other historical giants like Dante, Galileo, and Machiavelli, also hail from this dazzling city that gave rise to Europe's cultural rebirth after the Dark Ages. Many of the masterpieces most of us have only seen in schoolbooks are to be found right here. On top of that, there is ample cosmopolitan comforts to be found in this city − lovely gardens, the best gelato parlors, and some of the most delicious food you will have in Italy.

But once your eyes simply cannot absorb any more urban artistic beauty, leave the capital of Tuscany behind, and venture into the countryside. Remember *Under the Tuscan Sun*? The real Tuscany is only more beautiful − from endless fertile fields of grapes in Chianti, to the ancient hill city of San Gimignano in the shade of ancient olive groves. It is no wonder people have been making this area home for thousands of years. Who would not want to live in such natural abundance, such perfect loveliness?

Distinct from the rest of Italy, Florence and the Tuscany is a unique experience, a once-in-a-lifetime experience. With this pocket guide in hand, enjoy your trip to Florence and the Tuscany!

HOW TO USE THIS GUIDE

This pocket guide is centered around **Florence**, and radiates from the beautiful city into the equally beautiful **Tuscany** region. You'll want to start in the city proper, of course, perhaps coming from either **Rome** or **Venice** on your first tour of Italy. For more information on this route, see our book **Best of Italy**.

We introduce here all the most important sights and experiences in Florence, along with some signature eats and hotels we want to recommend. Plan your own days using these resources, or, if you are feeling lazy (it's a vacation after all!), just follow our 3-day itinerary in Florence. After you have drunk your fill of Renaissance arts and architecture in Florence, head on out to the countryside. You could rent a car and drive, or take the public transit options we give you at the end of each city's section.

Our 5-day itinerary, built on the 3-day itinerary in Florence, gives you ample time and opportunity to explore – wherever your interest may lie. For wine lovers, for example, we recommend taking a scenic drive into the **Chianti** region on your way to **Siena**, and stop by **Greve** for a tour of a vineyard. History lovers may wish to stop by the medieval towns of **San Gimignano or Montepulciano**. Or, if in the mood for something quaint, try **Lucca** with its sturdy city walls.

Top Experiences in Florence and Tuscany

1. Relive the Thriving Age of the Renaissance in Florence

In Florence, the cradle of the entire Renaissance period, you'll not have eyes enough to take in all the masterpieces by artists you've read about in your history textbooks. From Botticelli to Michelangelo, and of course, Leonardo da Vinci – the masters are all right here in Florence.

Florence

2. Visit Siena, and Catch the Il Palio Horserace

The town of Siena, with its architecture of sunshine yellows, bright oranges, and of course, the famous red that gave rise to the color "siena", is as nourishing for the soul as the Tuscan sun. If you are lucky, you might catch the twice-yearly horserace, about which the locals are as passionate as Italians elsewhere are about soccer.

3. Visit a Medieval Hill Town, like San Gimignano or Montepulciano

These charming towns, built into the Tuscan hillside, offer a glimpse into life of an earlier era. Their architecture, along with the locals' way of life, has remained largely unchanged. Montepulciano is also known for its wine.

4. Wine Tasting In Chianti

Famous for the white wine named after it, Chianti is one of the top destinations for the wine lover. Visit a vineyard, and at the end of the tour, sample some of the vineyard's produce, all while being surrounded by the beautiful vista of the Tuscan countryside.

Tuscany Area

5. Walk the Ancient City Walls of Lucca

Our favorite polymath, Leonardo da Vinci, designed the fortifications surrounding the ancient city of Lucca. Walk along the rampart is an activity both children and adults love. Great views are on hand, whichever direction you look!

6. Take a Photo of You Pushing the Leaning Tower of Pisa Up

Arguably one of the most famous towers in the world, the Leaning Tower of Pisa draws millions of visitors to this little Tuscan town. The must-have photo is of course a cleverly-angled shot of you trying to push the tower up.

7. La Dolce Vita!

Il dolce far niente – "the sweetness of doing nothing" is an art form the Italians have long learned to master. So when in Italy, do as the Italians do – bask in the Tuscan sun, celebrate life's pleasures, relax and let the sweetness of life sink in. Eat well, drink well, admire the beauty all around you, and enjoy!

Best of Florence and Tuscany Itineraries

3-Day Itinerary

Day 1

Spend all morning at the Duomo, before having lunch at Mercato Centrale nearby.

In the afternoon, visit the Piazza della Signoria, and the adjacent Palazzo Vecchio. Afterward, head to the nearby Uffizi Gallery in the late afternoon – you can avoid long lines by visiting after 4PM just before the gallery close.

Have dinner nearby. Grab a gelato after dinner, and take a walk on the Piazza della Signoria, where there's usually wonderful live music at night.

Day 2

If you're an art fan, take the morning to visit the Accademia for more Renaissance masterpieces, including Michelangelo's David.

Head to Ponte Vecchio, explore the shops on it. Visit the Pitti Palace or Boboli Gardens. Admire the panoramic view of Florence at Piazzale Michelangelo at sunset.

Day 3

The entire region of Tuscany is beautiful – filled with delicious food, gorgeous scenery, and art and architecture to rival Florence itself. We highly recommend a day trip to Siena.

This medieval town boasts of distinct architecture, and a more rustic vista than Florence. Twice a year, Siena hosts Il Palio – its ancient horse race that the locals are very passionate about. Visit for a more authentic "Italian" experience that you may not get in cities where tourism is more developed.

5-Day Itinerary

Day 1 and Day 2
See above.

Day 3
Travel to Pisa for the day, and visit the famous Leaning Tower.

Alternatively, visit Lucca for its quaint and winding roads.

Wine aficionados can go to Chianti instead, and tour some vineyards.

Day 4
Go to Siena (see above), and spend the night here for easy access to the hill towns.

Day 5
Take a bus from Siena to either San Gimignano for art, or Montepulciano for wine.

Traveling to other parts of Italy too? Plan the rest of your itinerary with Wanderlust Pocket Guide's **Best of Italy, Best of Rome, or Best of Venice**.

FLORENCE

Florence is the capital city of the Tuscany region in Italy, and one of the country's major cultural, artistic, and architectural gems. From the 1300's to the 1500's, it was the most important city in Europe politically, economically, and culturally, eventually fostering the birth of the Italian Renaissance. Florentines were also the inventors of money in the form of the gold florin, Renaissance and neoclassical architecture, and the opera.

The city was also the seat of the all-powerful Medicis, arguably the most important family in European history, having single-handedly taught the European countries how to conduct statecraft. Then there were the art they sponsored and helped flourish. Without them, and indeed without many of the famous Florentine artists – Botticelli, Piero della Francesca, Michelangelo, and of course, Leonardo da Vinci – the walls of some of the world's best museums today might just look very different.

Sights

Santa Maria del Fiore (Duomo di Firenze)
This most iconic of Florentine cathedrals has become synonymous with the city itself. The huge dome designed by Brunelleschi was a celebrated engineering feat of the Renaissance age. You can scale to the top of the dome, which has 464 steps. A statue of the architect can be found in the piazza outside, looking upwards toward his astonishing achievement.

Giotto's Tower
The tower, located next to the Duomo, offers a magnificent panoramic view of Florence and the surrounding areas. There are 414 steps to the top, so take your physical health into consideration before embarking on the climb.

Museo dell'Opera del Duomo
Just behind the Duomo is this cathedral museum, which hosts artworks that have occupied the Duomo and surrounding religious buildings in Florentine history, including sculptures by Donatello, a different version of the Pieta by Michelangelo that is in St. Peter's Basilica in the Vatican City, and, most amusingly, losing entries in the in the famous 1401 contest to design the doors of the Baptistery. There are also models and drawings of the cathedral from before it was constructed. Well worth the €6 entrance fee!

Galleria degli Uffizi
Some of the world's most famous Renaissance paintings and sculptures from antiquity are housed at the Galleria degli Uffizi,

including Botticelli's The Birth of Venus and Primavera, and Titian's Venus of Urbino. Avoid long lines by going in the afternoon, a few hours before the museum closes, or pay a bit extra to reserve online for immediate entry: http://www.b-ticket.com/b-ticket/uffizi/default.aspx.

Academia Gallery

Michaelangelo's well-known masterpieces David, and the unfinished Slaves, can both be found at the Academia.

Palazzo Vecchio

The one time city hall and palace of Florence, Palazzo Vecchio is now a museum adorned with fine art. A replica of Michelangelo's David is placed outside, at the statue's original location. There is also a big collection of Renaissance sculptures and paintings. The da Vinci masterpiece, Battaglia di Anghiari, used to be displayed here as well, but is now sadly lost.

The "fake" David outside of Palazzo Vecchio

Piazza della Signoria

Home to Palazzo Vecchio, Piazza della Signoria has its own claim to fame – the abundance of statues located all around the plaza, including, most famously, a copy of Michaelangelo's David. Other than Palazzo Vecchio, the plaza is also a good spot to rest your wary feet, have a cup of coffee at one of the cafes, or shop for a bit.

Piazza della Signoria at Night

Pitti Palace

Pitti was once the residence of the Medici family, and now serves as a museum for the art and treasures they collected. Behind the building, you can find the Boboli gardens with its wonderful walks, and views of the city as well as the countryside to the south.

Ponte Vecchio

Ponte Vecchio
This famous bridge stretching across the Arno is the only Florentine bridge to have survived World War II. Today, it is lined with shops – mostly jewelers, as it was during the days of the Medici.

Michelangelo Square (Piazzale Michelangelo)
Sitting atop a hill, Michelangelo Square offers the best panoramic view of the city. There is also a copy of Michelangelo's David. You may climb the stairs called "Rampe di San Niccoo" in front of the National Library, or take the bus to reach the top. This is a great spot to watch the sun set over the entire city.

View of Florence from Piazzale Michelangelo

Basilica di Miniato al Monte
Further uphill from PIazzale Michelangelo is the Basilica di Miniato al Monte, where the Sacristy contains frescoes by Spinello Aretino, and the cemetery contains graves of many famous residents of the city, including that of Carlo Lorenzi (also known as Collodi), author of the famous children's tale Pinocchio. Around service time at 6PM, you'll hear the monks' peaceful chant, a transcendent moment.

Basilica di Santa Croce
Here in Basilica di Santa Croce lays Galileo, Michelangelo, Machiavelli, Dante, and many other famous Italians from bygone eras. These monumental tombs are often elaborate and decorated in bas-relieves that point to their owners' life achievements. The church itself is generously decorated with great artwork.

After admiring the resting places of the Italian notables, you can buy a separate ticket to the Museo dell'Opera di Santa Croce, where you can see the beautiful crucifix by Cimabue, who was the teacher of the more famous Giotto. The crucifix, as you'll see, has suffered water damages in the 1966 flood, but has become a symbol of the event as well as the recovery of the city. Also within the basilica, you'll find the Pazzi Chapel, which is a perfectly symmetrical example of neo-Classic Renaissance architecture.

Church of Santa Maria Novella
Located near the main train station in Florence, the beautiful Church of Santa Maria Novella contains a range of great artwork, including most notably, a restored Trinity by Masaccio. Also, when you enter the church, to the right of you is the Chiostro Verde, which contains frescoes by Paolo Ucello, which possess a very unique style that you'd be sorry to miss. Toward the cloister of the church, there is the wonderful Spanish Chapel that is covered in early-Renaissance frescoes.

Museo Nazionale del Bargello
The Bargello Museum is home to some of the best-known examples of Renaissance mannerist sculpture in existence today, including great works by Michelangelo, Donatello, Ammannati, Bandinelli, Andrea, and Jacopo Sansovino, Desiderio da Settignano, Giambologna, and Antonio Rosselino. The museum is small enough to be seen in a few hours, for €11.50.

Gucci Museum
Milan may be Italy's fashion capital, but Florence is where influential brand Gucci chose to open its museum. Stop by for a few hours at the building on Piazza Signoria, and look through a collection of all the original styles created by the Italian tastemaker, founded by Guccio Gucci. There is also a café, restaurant, bookstore, and of course, a real Gucci store where you can buy vintage items.

Experience

Take a Walking Tour of Florence

Learn more about the city's illustrious history as you walk about this compact and exquisite city. Nearly every building boasts of hundreds of years of history, and its own fascinating backstory.

Watch Street Performers in front of the Palazzo Vecchio
In the evenings, street performers set up in front of Palazzo Vecchio, and attract a good crowd. Performances can range from violin duets to people masquerading as sculptures. It's a nice place to take an after-dinner walk.

Eat and Drink

Traditional hearty Tuscan fare, like the enormous Florentine steak, can be readily found in Florence. Also try lampredotto if you dare, a Florentine fast food dish using cow tripe that has a thousand years of history.

Florence also boasts of possibly the best gelato in all of Italy. It is usually freshly made in the bar where you buy it, and you can try many exotic flavors like watermelon, spumante, or garlic! Florentines eat dinner rather late – between 7PM to 9PM – and most gelato places will be closed by then, so consider having dessert first, before dinner.

Mercato Centrale is a large market that sells affordable fresh food on the ground floor, selling everything from fruits and vegetables to cheese and olive oil. The second floor has many cheap food stalls, with some seating in the middle. It's a great place to find affordable food and drinks.

The local liquor of choice is Chianti, which is pretty cheap at many Florentine eateries, with their own "house Chianti".

Aurelio il Re del Lampredotto
$
Tuscan

This tiny food stand just off Piazza Pietro Leopoldo offers reportedly the best lampredotto in all of Florence. Just three euros for a panino filled with piping hot tripe and a delicious spicy sauce? Yes, please!

Address: Piazza Bernardo Tanucci SNC, 50134 Florence, Italy

Panini Toscani
$
Sandwich

Close to the Museo Opera del Duomo, this sandwich restaurant is a great spot for lunch between sightseeing. The owner is very friendly, and lets you sample his entire meat and cheese selection before deciding what to order.

Address: Piazza Del Duomo 34/R | Close to Museo Opera Del Duomo, 50122 Florence, Italy

All'Antico Vinaio
$
Sandwich

A short walk from Uffizi Gallery, All'Antico Vinaio is practically a Florentine institution. Both locations, right across the street from each other, usually have long lines, and everyone eats squatting on the sidewalk. But the sandwich shop is still beyond amazing for its five-euro sandwiches, made with freshly baked bread crammed full with flavorful top-notch ingredients.

Address: Via De' Neri 65/R 74 /76/R | Via Dee Neri 65/R 74/R 76/R, 50122 Florence, Italy

Salumeria Verdi
$
Sandwich

Another fantastic panini spot with a menu full of 3.50-euro delights, Salumeria Verdi is also known for Pino, its proprietor and the friendly man with a camera-ready smile you'll find behind the counter!

Address: Via Giuseppe Verdi, 36/r, 50122 Florence, Italy

L'Pizzacchiere
$
Pizza

Tiny place, huge flavors! At the foot of the hill from Piazzale Michelangelo, this pizzeria might just serve you the best pizza of your life. You can also have a beer or a glass of local wine with your pie. It's unpretentious, but try to make a reservation ahead of time. It's that popular!
Address: Via   S.   Miniato   1/2 | Dinanzi   Al Rifrullo, 50125 Florence,Italy

La Prosciutteria
$$
Italian

You come to La Prosciutteria to have meat, cheese, and wine, and do they have lots of each! A whole night can be whiled away here, just nibbling on a little bit of cheese, a little bit of meat, washed down with a little bit of wine – then repeat! Great, fun atmosphere too.
Address: Via dei Neri 54r, 50122 Florence, Italy

Il Desco
$$
Italian

Try not to go back to this little restaurant night after night, we dare you. It's that good! The chef lovingly prepares locally sourced, fresh ingredients in the traditional Tuscan way. You would never believe veggies could taste so good.
Address: Cavour 27, 50129 Florence, Italy

La Buchetta Cafe
$$$
Italian, Pasta

A nice walk away from the Duomo and other major attractions, La Buchetta offers friendly service, and a range of amazing pasta, all cooked to traditional Italian perfection. The chocolate cake is pretty incredible too!

Address: Via De' Benci 3/3a, 50122 Florence, Italy

Cacio Vino Trallalla
$$$
Italian

Many visitors claim the best meal of their entire European vacation was right here in this unpretentious restaurant with just four tables. So make a reservation now, and give yourself the pleasure of eating the hearty yet still refined cuisine here.
Address: Borgo SS. Apostoli 29R, 50123 Florence, Italy

Enoteca Pitti Gola e Cantina
$$$$
Italian, Wine Bar

Located right in front of Pitti Palace, this little enoteca with an understated front is definitely not another tourist trap. Those in the know come here for a great Tuscan meal paired with great Tuscan wine. If you want to learn a bit more about the local cuisine and wines, book a "Dinner with Owner" ahead of time online. You'll be treated to a meal with one of the three brothers who own the place, while they explain everything that is served. A great place worth of a splurge!
Address: Piazza Pitti 16, 50125 Florence, Italy

Stay

Hotel David
Address: Viale Michelangiolo, 1, 50125 Florence, Italy

Portrait Firenze
Address: Viale Michelangiolo, 1, 50125 Florence, Italy

Palazzo Castri 1874
Address: Piazza dell_Indipendenza, 7, 50129 Florence, Italy

Villa Cora
Address: Viale Niccolo Machiavelli 18, 50125 Florence, Italy

Hotel Spadai
Address: Via Dei Martelli 10, 50129 Florence, Italy

Antica Torre di Via Tornabuoni
Address: Via dei Tornabuoni 1, 50122 Florence, Italy

Ville sull'Arno Hotel
*Address: Lungarno Cristoforo Colombo
1/3/5, 50136 Florence, Italy*

Hotel Davanzati
Address: Via Porta Rossa no 5, 50123 Florence, Italy

Firenze Number Nine Hotel & Spa
Address: Via dei Conti, 9/31R, 50123 Florence, Italy

Torre Di Bellosguardo
Address: 2 Via Roti Michelozzi, 50124 Florence, Italy

Palazzo Magnani Feroni
Address: Borgo San Frediano, 5, 50124 Florence, Italy

Golden Tower Hotel & Spa
Address: Piazza Strozzi 11r, 50123 Florence, Italy

Hotel Brunelleschi
*Address: Piazza Santa Elisabetta 3 | Via De
Calzaioli, 50122 Florence, Italy*

Getting In

By Train
Fast trains from other major Italian cities, express trains from around Europe, and local trains from other parts of Italy, all connect to Firenze Santa Maria Novella, the very centrally located main train station in Florence. For example, the speed train from

either Venice or Rome gets you to Florence in around 2 hours – very convenient.

By Air

If you choose to fly into Florence, you'll land in Amerigo Vespucci International Airport, commonly known as Peretola. From there, the Ataf-Sita "Vola in Bus" ("Fly by Bus), which costs €6.00 one-way, runs to the train station Firenze Santa Maria Novella every half hour from 5:30AM to 8PM, then once an hour for the rest of the time. Alternatively, you can take a flat-rate cab for €25, which will take you from the airport to any location in the historic center of the city. Luggage handled by the driver is €1 per piece.

Getting Around

Florence is a very walking-friendly city, especially where major tourist sights are concerned. A walk through the entire historic center takes about half an hour, and not only gets you to the attractions, but lets you take in more of the essence of Florence.

Alternatively, you can rent a bike from various city-organized services around town. The most convenient location for visitors is usually Firenze Santa Maria Novella station. While hills to the north and south of the town center may be hard to negotiate for bikers, most of the historic center of Florence is on flat land, and very easy to bike – if you don't count the terrible traffic.

There is also a public bus service in Florence. A single, €1.2 ticket, is valid for 90 minutes, and can be bought from the tobacco shop right outside the main train station, or at any kiosks with the symbol "Biglietti ATAF". You can choose to get a day ticket for €5, a three-day ticket for €12, a four-ride ticket for €4.50. A batch of 10 tickets is €12, and a batch of 35 is €36 – perfect for a large group.

Savings Pass

Visitors to Florence may choose to buy a "Firenze Card", which gives you access to 30 museums and free use of the public transit system. At some museums, you can also skip the reservations procedure with the pass, but it is prudent to check ahead with individual museums. The pass costs €72, and can be bought online: http://www.firenzecard.it/.

Siena

Located just a short train ride from Florence, the Tuscan city of Siena was a wealthy Medieval city-state known today for Il Palio, its world famous horse race conducted twice a year in the summer. The city's contribution to art and architecture is quite unique, and of no less importance than Florence.

During Il Palio

Sights

Siena Cathedral (Siena Duomo)
The stately black and white Siena Cathedral includes the Liberia Piccolomini Baptistery, and an attached Museum dell'Opera del Duomo, where you can see the famous Maesta by Duccio. After you've seen the art, ascend to Il Facciatone in the museum for a panorama of the city.

Piazza del Campo

The piazza at the city center is shell shaped, and twice a year serves as the racetrack for Il Palio.

Mangia Tower (Torre del Mangia)
This 88 meter tall tower, built to the exact height of the Siena Cathedral as a sign that church and state wield equal power in the city of Siena, offers amazing views, but is a bit tough to hike its 300 steps, not to mention claustrophobic, as only 25 people are allowed into the cramped staircase at a time. But once you are at the top, the view will make you forget all of that.

Palazzo Pubblico
This palazzo served as Siena's city hall for almost 800 years, through its proud lineage. The museum now contains the famous frescos on good and bad government by Ambrogio Lorenzetti, frescoes by Simone Martini and Duccio. It is also where you would access the Mangia Tower.

Experience

Il Palio
Siena's famous horse race is about more than just racing horses, strangely. It has a lot to do with the city's neighborhood pride and rivalry, and represents a continuation of traditions of religion, pageantry, trash-talking, bragging, and occasional violence, passed down from Medieval times. Unlike in more touristy cities, Siena is not putting on this race for the tourists' enjoyment – in fact, you may feel least welcomed during the Palio than at any other time. This is a Siennese tradition, one the city treasures.

There are currently 17 contrades participating in the two annual horse races, on July 2 and August 16. All locals are affiliated with one of the teams, and feel such loyalty to their team that puts even an avid football fan to shame. At some point, in addition to horse races, there were also fist fights – something like soccer hooligans getting into trouble with one another – but heavy police presence has put a stop to that particular tradition.

Wine Tours
The entire region of Tuscany is renowned for winemaking. As such, you can book a wine tour into the countryside from many Tuscan cities, including Siena.

Eat and Drink

A Siennese classic is panforte, a dense cake made of honey, flour, almonds, candied fruits, and a secret blend of spices. It is only commercially made in Siena and the nearby city of Monteriggioni. The most ubiquitous brand is Sapori, which you can get readily in local supermarkets. But if you can, stop by cafes like Nannini on Banchi di Sopra, where you can have fresh panforte and other regional pastries, and buy some for people back home before you leave!

La Prosciutteria
$
Wine Bar
Perfect little spot for a mid-afternoon snack of Tuscan cheese and sausages, with a glass of wine.
Address: Via Pantaneto | Angolo Via Magalotti, 53100 Siena, Italy□□□□□□□□□□

Menchetti
$
Pizza
Some of the best pizza in Siena, and very good value!
Address: Via Giuseppe Pianigiani, 5, 53100 Siena, Italy□□□□□□□□□□

Gino Cacino di Angelo
$$
Italian

Try a sandwich, or the massive platter of meat and cheese the proprietor Angelo is famous for!

Address: Piazza Del Mercato 31, 53100 Siena, Italy□□□□□□□□□□

Osteria La Sosta di Violante
$$
Italian

The tagliata at this osteria has been described as "transcendent", and "the best to be had in Italy".

Address: Via Di Pantaneto 115, 53100 Siena, Italy□□□□□□□□□□

Ristorante San Domenico
$$$
Italian

This restaurant is the opposite of a tourist trap – large portions, reasonably priced, beautifully cooked local fare all served with by friendly locals.

Address: Via Camporegio 17, 53100 Siena, Italy□□□□□□□□□□

Antica Osteria da Divo
$$$
Italian

Seated in an ancient Etruscan wine cellar, you are treated to Tuscan delicacies with a refined twist at Antica OSteria da Divo.

Address: Via Franciosa 25-29, Siena, Italy□□□□□□□□□□

La Taverna di San Giuseppe
$$$$
Tuscan

Enjoy some classic Tuscan fare at this quaint but upscale restaurant. It's drawn many patrons among visitors to Siena over the years, and making some repeat customers on a second trip!

Address: Via Giovanni Dupre 132, 53100 Siena, Italy□□□□□□□□□□

Getting In

The best way to reach Siena is by taking a one-hour train from Florence, which lets you off at the train station about 2 kilometers from the historical center. A five-minute bus ride gets you between the station and Piazza del Sale.

SAN GIMIGNANO

The quaint town of San Gimignano, surrounded by medieval walls, makes a great day trip if you are Siena or Florence, for its beautiful towers and great art.

Sights

San Gimignano Bell Towers
There are a total of 14 towers standing in the town today, out of the original 72 which were built by the wealthy when the town was sacked by Florence. Many were torn down when the city came under Florentine control.

Torre Grossa is the tallest vantage point in the city at 200 feet. A ticket will get you to the top of the tower for stunning views of the town and surrounding Tuscany vista, and into the Pinacoteca Civica museum.

Piazza del Duomo

The town's main square, presided over by the church of the city, is surrounded by the famous thousand-year-old towers.

Piazza della Cisterna

The focal point of this beautiful piazza is an old stone well that locals used to retrieve water in ancient times. While the well is no longer in use today, the square hosts a market every Thursday, and is home to some of the best restaurants in the town.

San Gimignano 1300 Museum

Located in town center, this museum contains a massive reconstruction of the city of San Gimignano as it was during the 13th and 14th century. Entrance is free, so don't miss this opportunity to learn about the town's architectural and cultural heritage, and that of the surrounding area in Tuscany.

Eat

Gelateria Dondoli
$
Dessert
Amazing gelato worthy of its reputation – you simply cannot miss Dondoli on a trip to San Gimignano.
Address: Piazza della Cisterna, 4, 53037 San Gimignano, Italy

Echoes
$
Pub
Serving tasty small plates with plenty of Tuscan wine, Echoes is an off-the-beaten-path gem you are sure to love.
Address: Vicolo Mainardi 10, 53037 San Gimignano, Italy

Le Vecchie Mura

$
Italian
Along with amazing food, Le Vecchie Mura offers an equally amazing view of San Gimignano from its terrace.
Address: via Piandornella, 15, San Gimignano, Italy□□□□□□□□□□

Café Giardino
$$
Italian
There are only 6 tables at the café, but score one, and you'll be treated to a never-ending parade of fresh food curated by Giardino himself.
Address: Viale Roma 17 | In the Square Outside S. Giovanni Gate, 53037 San Gimignano, Italy□□□□□□□□□□

Cum Quibus
$$$$
Italian
Traditional Tuscan fare is served with an international Michelin-star flair.
Address: Via San Martino, 17, 53037 San Gimignano, Italy□□□□□□□□□□

Getting In

To reach the hill town of San Gimignano, you can take a train from Florence, disembark at Poggibonsi, and change to a bus that takes you to San Gimignano. Alternatively, there are direct buses from Florence or Siena, which might take a bit longer.

LUCCA

Well-preserved Renaissance walls, topped by broad, tree-lined pathways along the massive ramparts, encircle the historic city of Lucca, situated right on River Serchio in Italy's Tuscany region. Walls designed by non other than Leonardo da Vinci, that most impressive polymath whose defensive fortifications here were never breached – unlike other city-states in the region that were steadily absorbed by more major powers like Florence, Lucca remained independent until the end of the 18th century. Today, the top of these walls form a ring park, enclosing the old city center, where can take a delightful stroll, while looking down at the city's ancient ruins from Etruscan and Roman times, as well as the marvelous architecture that the Gothic and Renaissance eras left.

Opera aficionados may also have heard of Lucca as the birthplace of Giacomo Puccini, one of the most famous Italian opera composers to date.

Sights

Lucca's City Walls

Leonardo da Vinci's walls must have been superiorly designed, as the walls enclosing Lucca's historic old city are some of the best-preserved ramparts you'll find anywhere in Italy. These more than four kilometers of walls, with six gates and eleven bastions, have been planted with trees and grass, turning the defensive measure into a huge park. You can walk all around the city, or even ride a bike on top of the wall!

Roman Amphitheater (Piazza dell'Anfiteatro)

This oval shaped piazza was once the site of a Roman amphitheater in the second century. Today, you can still see parts of the original ground-plan, and an outer ring of construction, but more modern buildings and houses have been steadily built around the arena since the Middle Ages. Our own time has seen the addition of a number of shops, cafes, and restaurants spring up both inside and out of the ancient ground. In July, you'll find many open-air music performances taking place.

Duomo (Cathedrale di San Martino)

Even amid all the impressive medieval buildings similarly located on Piazza San Martino, the Cathedral of Lucca, dedicated to San Martino, is a stunning sight. It possesses an intricate marble façade, in the Romanesque style, and is flanked by its tall bell tower, both built in the 12th to 13th century. The interior is decorated in Gothic style, and contains a number of important artworks, including the Volto Santo, and Ilaria del Carretto, a 15th century tomb piece designed by Jacopo della Quercia.

On the other side and around the piazza, you'll find many medieval houses typical to Lucca. The one next to the cathedral is appropriately known as Casa dell'Opera del Duomo.

Torre Guinigi

At the top of the 130 stairs of the Guinigi Tower, built in the 14th century, are large Holm oaks, strangely growing out of the top, and the best view to be had of the entire city of Lucca as well as the surrounding countryside. Located on via Guinigi, the tower is neighbor to Case del Giunigi, a complex of 14th century towers and brick houses.

San Michele in Foro Church

In the time of the Roman Empire, the square on which San Michele in Foro Church is located was the Forum at the center of the city. Today, the square has many medieval buildings that have been converted into cafes, shops, and restaurants, where you can sit and have a coffee. The church itself, with its beautiful marble façade in the Romanesque style that is interestingly larger than the actual church building, is recognizable for the large statue of the archangel San Michele, that sits atop its roof.

San Frediano Church

Originally built in the 6th century, but remodeled in the 12th century, San Frediano Church has a façade decorated with intricate 13th century Byzantine-style gold leaf mosaics that dazzle the eye in the sunlight. The baptismal font inside is in the Romanesque style, and there are several good artworks and frescoes to be seen, alongside the mummified body of Santa Zita.

Experiences

Walk the Walls

Walk the 4 kilometers perimeter of the city walls, and you'll be treated to a special view of the city and its ancient layout.

Listen to masterful works of Puccini

Having given birth to the great master of opera, Puccini, Lucca now regularly hosts young opera singers from across Europe and North America, especially during the summer months, for its many opera festivals.

Eat and Drink

Buccellato, a sweetbread in the shape of a small baguette or a bun, with raisins and seasoned by anise, is Lucca's local specialty and only to be found here. Try it at a little shop behind Saint Michael's church in the main square, called Taddeucci.

La Tana del Boia
$
Sandwich
Excellent sandwiches, cheese and meat plates, all served with craft ales.
Address: Piazza San Michele 37, 55100 Lucca, Italy□□□□□□□□□□

Le Bonta
$
Dessert
Le Bonta's gelato gives Grom in Florence a serious run for its money. There is even a bakery attached if you want some lovely Tuscan pastries instead.
Address: Via C.Castracani 269 Arancio, 55100 Lucca, Italy□□□□□□□□□□

Da Pasquale
$$
Italian
The owner is very generous, and often wants to share a glass of locally produced wine with his patrons.
Address: Via Del Moro, 8, 55100 Lucca, Italy□□□□□□□□□□□

Allosteria
$$$
Italian
Allosteria offers a stylish modern menu that updates the traditional Tuscan food – very refreshing from the usual fare.

Address: Via S. Andrea, 8 | Lucca Centro Vicino Torre Guinigi, 55100 Lucca, Italy☐☐☐☐☐☐☐☐☐☐

Getting In

You can take the train from either Pisa Central Station, or from Florence. The station is just outside the old town walls.

PISA

Most visitors come to Pisa just to see the famous Leaning Tower, but it'd be a huge mistake to miss the rest of the beautiful city!

Sights

Piazza dei Miracoli
The piazza will undoubtedly be your first stop in Pisa. This UNESCO World Heritage site contains the Leaning Tower, as well as most other important attractions in the city.

Leaning Tower of Pisa (Torre Pendente)
We don't need to tell you to come see the Leaning Tower. The famous structure was originally planned as the bell tower for Pisa Cathedral. It started leaning soon after construction began in 1173, due to subsidence of the ground beneath. The tower was closed for a while but a project to keep it from toppling over reached a successful conclusion in 2001, so now you may climb to the top once again.

You'll need to reserve a specific time to climb the tower, which is usually 45 minutes to 2 hours after purchase time, but there are plenty of other sights on the piazza alone to occupy you during that time.

Fun fact: while the Tower of Pisa is the most famous, there are two other leaning towers – the Bell Tower of San Nicola Church, and the Bell Tower of San Michele of Scalzi Church, that also lean due to the marsh soil they are built on.

Leaning Tower of Pisa

Pisa Cathedral (Duomo di Pisa)

The city cathedral of Pisa contains artwork by major artists like Giambologna and Della Robbia. The beautiful Romanesque structure with double aisles and a cupola, a huge apse mosaic partially by Cimabue, and a fine pulpit by Giovanni Pisano, is full of surprising delights.

45

Campo Santo Monumentale (Monumental Cemetery)

Like many Italian cemeteries, this building in Pisa is more of a gallery with its collection of ancient Roman sarcophagi, and splendid medieval frescoes by the "Master of the Triumph of Death".

Battistero (Baptistry)

Climb to the dome of this building, and you'll be treated to a great view of the Leaning Tower. The interior of the Battistero features many sculptured decorations, an Arabic-style pavement, pulpit by Nicola Pisano, and fine octagonal font. The acoustics at this building are ingenious – at regular intervals, the ticket checker will come inside, and shout out a few sounds which when echoed, turn into a few beautiful notes from the most delightful music. If you are not shy, try it yourself by standing by the wall, and sing long notes that reverberate into harmonic chords as the echoes travel round and round in the dome at the top.

Experiences

Luminara Festival

Once a year on June 16th, Pisa pays respect to its patron saint – San Ranieri, with the Luminara festival. At sunset, all lights along the Arno are dimmed, and replaced by more than 10,000 candles. It's a stunning sight from the Ponte di Mezzo. The night is completed by activities on the street, and end with a big firework show.

Spa Day

Casciana Terme has served as a thermal bath since ancient times. Many of the water's healing powers are just in recent years being studied, but no scientific inquiry is necessary to enjoy the relaxing atmosphere after a long day of sightseeing.

Eat and Drink

Gusto Giusto
$
Sandwich
Proprietor Giusto will fix you any sandwich (they are all amazing) you want from his large selection of meats and cheeses for around five euros!

Address: Via Cottolengo, 25 | traversa corso italia, 56125 Pisa, Italy□□□□□□□□□□

L'Ostellino
$
Sandwich
This restaurant off of the main street is a great lunch place with an amazing platter meet and cheese platter.

Address: Piazza Cavallotti,1, 56126 Pisa, Italy□□□□□□□□□□□

Gusto al. 129 Pizzeria
$
Pizza
This unpretentious little place serves all sorts of delicious pizza, even one for dessert.

Address: Via Santa Bibbiana 10 | Monday Closed, 56127 Pisa, Italy□□□□□□□□□□

Getting In
Just like Siena, Pisa is just a one-hour long train ride away from Florence. The main train station is called Pisa Centrale, but to see the Leaning Tower, you should get off at the Pisa S. Rossore station, closer to the Tower and other attractions.

GREVE IN CHIANTI

When you head south from Florence, in the direction of Siena, the first major town you reach is Greve, the entrance gate to the Chianti region. Made famous by the red wine named in its honor, Chianti is rich in history and culture, natural beauty, and of course, acre after acre of rich soil that nourishes some of the best grapes in the world, and has been producing great wine since the days of the Roman Empire. In fact, "Chianti" is not an administrative region at all, but rather a "wine zone" that contains parts of the Tuscan provinces of Florence, Siena, Arezzo, and Pisa.

The township of Greve, from whose walls the entire region spreads out, is the perfect place to enjoy a cup of espresso, a gelato cone, or indeed, a glass of locally produced wine, as you drive through the beautiful countryside.

Chianti Region

Sights

Piazza Matteotti

So the oddly shaped piazza is not exactly a "square", but it is nonetheless the focal point of the town. If you are driving through Greve on your way to the wider Chianti region, park near here, and start exploring the museums and monuments on the square. For a true Chianti experience, enjoy a relaxing wall through the winding streets, and check out some of the food and wine festivals that are always happening in Greve, or stop and listen to the live music. The best time for taking advantage of all this liveliness is in the summer and early fall.

Every Saturday morning, the town market still meets on this same square as it has for centuries at least. Aside from its strange shape, the square is also surrounded by portico on three sides, which has and continues to serve as the frame for artisan shops, workshops, and restaurants, selling local products.

Experience

Of course, wine tasting is a must in Chianti. Here are some of the best wineries for a tour and some delicious wine tasting:

Montefioralle Winery
Via Montefioralle 45, 50022 Greve in Chianti,Italy

Castello di Verrazzano
Via Citille, 32, 50022 Greve in Chianti, Italy

Enoteca Falorni
Piazza Delle Cantine, 6, 50022 Greve in Chianti, Italy

Eat and Drink

The wine is not named after Chianti for no reason – when you visit the region, you will of course want to drink Chianti wine. Traditional Chianti is made with a base of sangiovese grapes, a rather difficult grape to grow, with fewer quantities of other grape varieties (including white ones) added to the producer's discretion. This results in a light wine with high acidity, and slightly bitter but fruity taste as well as berry aromas. In recent years, however, demand from international wine markets has caused Chianti to evolve to a certain degree, and more modern (high-fruit, high-alcohol) versions of this classic wine featuring a fuller, but less distinct taste, has emerged. You might just have to sample them all, and decide which you consider the best.

Getting In

The best and easiest way to move through and fully appreciate Chianti is by car. Via Chiantigiana from Florence to Siena, flanked by endless fields of grapevines, is one of the most scenic roads you'll drive through.

If you don't want to drive, grab Bus 365 from the SMN train station in Florence for a direct ride.

Montepulciano

The Tuscan city of Montepulciano is famous for its classic red wine, Vino Nobile di Montepulciano, considered one of Italy's best, among other well-made libations. It also produces great pork, cheese, "pici" pasta, lentils, and honey. Stop by for a day trip, and enjoy the laid-back hill town while treating yourself to a scrumptious meal.

Sights

Piazza Grande
A beautiful square surrounded by beautiful buildings on all sides, Piazza Grande should not be missed. You'll find the stunning architectural marvels of Palazzo Comunale, Contucci Palace, and Palazzo de' Nobili-Tarugi.

Climb to the top of the clock tower of Palazzo Comunale for a great view of the town, and enjoy a fun wine tasting in the basement of Contucci Palace, where the city's jail has been converted into a cantina.

Experiences

Avignonesi Winery
Situated on the border of Tuscany and Umbria, Avignonesi is a scenic hillside spot for wine tasting that includes a tour of the facilities, culminating in a delicious lunch, paired of course, with the wine produced on site.

Eat

Le Logge del Vignola
$$$
Italian

With just four tables of two each, Le Logge del Vignola is all about quality.

Address: Via delle Erbe, 6, 53045 Montepulciano, Italy□□□□□□□□□□□

Ristorante La Grotta
$$$$
Italian

Enjoy a lovely meal in the equally lovely garden of Ristorante la Grotta.

Address: Localita' San Biagio, 15, 53045 Montepulciano, Italy□□□□□□□□□□

Getting In

Take the train from Florence, and get off at Chiusi-Chianciano Terme. From there, take a taxi or a bus to Montepulciano, which should take around 50 minutes. There are buses from Siena directly to Montepulciano, but like all Italian buses, they are not the most reliable. You might be waiting for quite some time.

PLANNING YOUR TRIP

BEST TIME TO VISIT FLORENCE

July and August are when Italy is most crowded and expensive to visit, as many Italians and other Europeans are on vacation, driving prices high and queues at attractions long. The same applies for holidays like Christmas, New Year, and Easter.

The best times to visit are spring to early summer, or early fall. In general, in April to June, September to October, you should be able to score good deals on accommodation, especially in southern Italy. The weather is less hot and humid as well, making for a more enjoyable experience. In the spring, you'll see beautiful flowers and fresh local produce, as well as a number of festivals. In the autumn, you'll have warm, temperate weather, and grapes would have just been harvested at vineyards across the country.

November to March is low season. While prices will the cheapest, some sights and hotels in coastal and mountainous areas will be closed. This won't be a problem for major cities like Florence, however, where tourists surround attractions like the Duomo di Firenze year-round, even in terrible weather.

For Florence, early April is a safe bet, as the weather has not become too hot or too humid, but it is still warm enough for cafes and restaurants to open up their outdoor seating. In January and February, you won't have to battle the crowds, but it does get cold. August is a no-no, as Tuscany gets smolderingly hot, and most locals will have fled the city to go on vacation near the sea. Many shops and restaurants will be closed for this reason.

Note that museums in Florence are closed on certain days, most likely on Mondays, so it is best to check ahead.

Exchange Rates

Unit = Euro (€)

Rates are calculated at the time of this writing. Please check before your departure for the up-to-date exchange rate.

USD: 1 Dollar = 0.9 Euro
Canadian Dollar: 1 Dollar = 9.71 Euro
British Pounds: 1 Pound = 1.39 Euro
Australian Dollar: 1 Dollar = 0.67 Euro

Visa Information

Italy is a member of the Schengen agreement. There are no border controls between countries that have signed the treaty, so citizens from those countries can freely cross into Italy. Many non-EU countries are visa-exempt. Citizens from those countries will only need to produce a valid passport when entering the country, as the stamp counts as a declaration. For more information, visit the Italian Ministry of Foreign Affairs website: http://www.esteri.it/mae/en/ministero/servizi/stranieri/default.html.

US: eligible for visa-free stay, up to 90 days
Canada: eligible for visa-free stay, up to 90 days
Australia: eligible for visa-free stay, up to 90 days

ESSENTIAL ITALIAN CULTURE TO KNOW

Italians are in general very patriotic, though people from different regions are proud of their regional heritage as well. They are also more often than not open and friendly, and enjoy interacting with people of every kind. Paying compliments is generally a good way to make friends. For example, tell someone how beautiful his or her town is will work wonders, especially if you can compare their town favorably to another city.

Don't be shy about asking the locals for restaurant recommendations! Italy is filled with good food, and it would be a crime to eat at tourist traps instead of sampling authentic local cuisine. Very often, the locals can point you to their favorite spots off the beaten path, which will be cheaper and more tasty than what you can find on your own in the touristy areas.

Theft is a common problem, especially in large cities like Naples and Rome. Rome is full of pickpocket, though violent crimes are rare. In public areas, crowded metros and buses, hold onto your handbags and wallets. Men should avoid putting their wallets in their back pockets. You should also watch out for gypsies.

USEFUL ITALIAN TERMS AND PHRASES

In larger cities, you'll likely find someone who speaks English, but in a small town or less touristy areas, it'll be helpful to have some Italian phrases.

Do you speak English: Parla Inglese?

Thank You: Grazie.

You are welcome: Prego.

Please: Per favore; Per Piacere.

Good Morning/Good Afternoon: Buon Giorno.

Good Evening: Buona Sera.

Good Night: Buona note.

How are you (singular): Come sta?

How are you (plural): Come state?

Excuse me: Mi scusi/Scusi.

Hello/Goodbye: Ciao.

How much does it cost: Quanto costa?

Where is ...: Dov'è ....?

Lavatory/Toilet: Gabinetto/Bagno.

To eat: Mangiare

Where is the ... Embassy: Dove si trova... l'ambasciata?

Restaurant: Ristorante.

Stamp: Francobollo.

Postcard: Cartolina.

May I take photos: Posso fare fotografie?

Where can I find a...: Dove posso trovare un.../

I have a booking/we have a booking: Ho una prenotazione/Abbiamo una prenotazione.

Would like something to eat: Vorrei qualcosa da mangiare.

I would like something to drink: Vorrei qualcosa da bere.

How can I go to...: Come posso andare a...

I am allergic to...: Sono allergico a...

Do you accept credit cards: Accettate carte di credito?

Prescription: Prescrizione/Ricetta.

May I pay at check-out: Posso pagare al check-out?

Check please: Il conto, per favore.

Is there internet connection: C'è la connessione ad internet.

How much does it cost? / How much does this cost: Quanto costa? / Quanto costa questo?

Police: Polizia/Carabinieri.

Taxi: Taxi.

Bus stop: Fermata dell'autobus.

Airport: Aeroporto.

Train station: Stazione.

Pharmacy: Farmacia.

Doctor: Medico.

Hotel: Albergo/Hotel.

Pain: Dolore.

Blisters: Vesciche.

Food store: Supermercato.

Shop: Negozio.

Hospital: Ospedale.

Emergency room: Pronto soccorso.

Museum: Museo.

Ticket desk: Biglietteria.

Guidebook: Guida turistica.

Guided tour: Visita guidata.

Opening time: Orario di aperture.

Go away: Vai via!

CONCLUSION

We hope this pocket guide helps you navigate Florence and the Tuscany region, and find the most memorable and authentic things to do, see, and eat.

Thank you for purchasing our pocket guide. After you've read this guide, we'd really appreciate your honest book review!

Sincerely,
The Wanderlust Pocket Guides Team

PLANNING A TRIP OR SEEKING TRAVEL INSPIRATION?

Check out our other Wanderlust Pocket Guides on Amazon

Also available are our comprehensive day-to-day City Guides

CREDITS

Cover design by Wanderlust Pocket Guide Design Team

COPYRIGHT AND DISCLAIMER

Made in the USA
Lexington, KY
21 May 2016